Reflections on Humans and their Surroundings

Awareness, Experience, Qualia, Hearing, Memory, Perception, Thought, Freedom, Sensations, Character, Personality, Evolution, Technology, Science & Faith

Simon Saint

123 Books

A catalogue record for this book is available from the British Library

ISBN: 978-1-907962-01-1

Published by 123 Books

Reading, England

For Emma

Nothing ever is, everything is becoming

Plato on the views of Heraclitus[1]

*Knowing ignorance is strength. Ignoring knowledge
is sickness.*

Lao Tse[2]

---

[1] Russell, Bertrand, *History of Western Philosophy*, George
Allen & Unwen Ltd., London, 2004, p. 52.

[2] Lao Tse, *Tao Te Ching*, Vintage Books, New York, 1972.

Contents

Preface

This book is a collection of reflections concerning humans and their surroundings. The topics which are the subject of the individual reflections are those which I personally find to be of great interest and importance. They are also topics which I believe I might have something to say which could possibly be of interest to you. You might not agree with all of my conclusions, but hopefully the reflections which follow will stimulate your own reflective processes and give you 'food for thought' concerning these topics.

Introduction

Reflections on Humans and their Surroundings

As the years, decades and centuries come and go humans gradually acquire more and more knowledge of the surroundings which engulf them. There was a time, a long time ago, when humans first developed a 'world view' – a view of how humans relate to their surroundings. As human knowledge of their surroundings gradually increases new human 'world views' are born. This is the normal state of affairs. Humans are born at a particular time, indoctrinated into an existing 'world view', and any significant advances in human knowledge that occur in one's lifetime can cause one to change one's 'world view'.

Of course, the usual state of affairs is for several 'world views' to exist at the same time. In other words, the 'world view' one is indoctrinated into could have been different if one was born into a different family or in a different country. Why are there several 'world views'? A preliminary answer is that for most of human history there hasn't been a common stock of human knowledge about the engulfing surroundings. This means that different 'world views' informed by varying degrees of knowledge would have emerged in different parts of the world. It is an interesting question whether the increasing globalization of knowledge will lead to a reduction in the number of 'world views' that exist. The answer is surely that such a reduction will occur.

Another point of crucial importance is that a 'world view' can also be forged through an individual experience which is so powerful that it causes a person to utterly reject the 'world view' into which they were indoctrinated and to adopt a radically different view. This means that whilst there are disparate 'world views' which have advanced gradually over the centuries, there are also times when a person can switch from one existing 'world view' to another, or even forge their own radically new 'world view'.

There are also occasions in which rare radical breakthroughs in the communal stock of human knowledge can cause a radical change in the 'world view' of a person. Whilst the breakthroughs are rare, the changes in 'world view' initiated by them are common.

So, whilst various human 'world views' gradually change over time, individuals can have radical changes in their individual 'world view' which are instantaneous. Can there be an instantaneous change in an entire 'world view'? That is to say: Can a particular 'world view' instantaneously be disregarded by every human who believes it. No – this isn't the way things work; in reality, even radical breakthroughs in knowledge concerning human surroundings take a very long time to be acknowledged and accepted. These breakthroughs tend to be deeply counterintuitive because they are typically opposed to the existing 'world views'. This means that the particular 'world views' that exist at a particular moment in time often exist alongside the knowledge that refutes them, and which ultimately leads to their replacement.

What is one to do when one realises that there are diverse 'world views' and that the current 'world view' one holds is almost certainly wrong? What is one to do when one realises the true extent of one's ignorance of one's surroundings? Initially, one can look for the knowledge that currently exists but which has not yet initiated a change in the existing 'world views'. At a deeper level one can attempt to free oneself from all 'world views' and to reflect on the possible relationships between oneself and one's engulfing surroundings. The following reflections make use of both of these approaches.

Reflection 1

Awareness, Experience & Qualia

Let us consider the phenomena of awareness, experience and qualia. How do these three phenomena relate to each other? Reflecting on this issue entails a number of tasks. The first task is to clarify the exact nature of the phenomena. The second task is to elucidate the various ways in which the phenomena could relate to each other. The third task is to ask the question: Is it possible to know how the phenomena actually relate to each other? If the answer to this question is no then a final task presents itself – assessing the arguments for the various possible ways in which the phenomena could possibly be related in order to assess whether a particular way is more attractive than the alternatives.

Task 1 – Clarifying the nature of the phenomena

What does it mean to say that awareness exists? It is certain that awareness exists because the existence of awareness provides awareness of existence. Awareness of existence exists and therefore awareness exists. Awareness of existence and awareness are one. Awareness cannot know for certain that it is not the only awareness of existence that exists – the possible existence of other parts of reality that are also aware of existence has to be inferred by awareness. Awareness knows that awareness exists because it exists.

What more can intelligibly be said about the phenomena of awareness? Whilst it is certain that awareness of existence exists, it is equally certain that awareness of existence ceases to exist. At one moment awareness of existence exists, the following moment it can vanish. Once awareness has vanished there are two possibilities – it may return to existence or it may be lost forever to the realms of inexistence. The first possibility occurs when awareness re-emerges following a period of sleep, and also when awareness re-emerges following its vanishing due to a sharp blow to the head. The second possibility occurs when the foundations which enable awareness to exist themselves cease to exist. It is the initial lack of these foundations which explains why awareness of existence emerges from the realms of inexistence. In the past the universe was wholly devoid of these foundations, then the foundations emerged which enabled awareness of existence to exist, to vanish, to re-emerge from inexistence, and finally to return wholly to inexistence.

What is to be said of dreaming? Obviously a prerequisite for dreaming is sleeping, and in sleep awareness of existence doesn't exist – awareness has vanished to the realms of inexistence. In a dream a delusion of awareness of existence can be generated – but this is clearly not awareness of existence. A dream can exist wherein there is a realistic appearance of being a soldier in World War I. Given that it is 2011 this appearance clearly doesn't entail awareness of existence. At one moment awareness doesn't exist – all that exists is a delusion of World War I – the next moment awareness of existence re-emerges, becomes aware of the bedroom surroundings, and remembering the delusion is relieved that it was a delusion and not awareness of existence. It wouldn't have been nice to be an awareness of existence that existed in the trenches of World War I. Of course, the experience of waking and recovering awareness of existence can itself be part of a dream. But anyone who denies that there are times when delusional dreams end and awareness of actual existence re-emerges would need to assert that all that exists is one exceptionally long dream, for everyone knows that there are times when they regain awareness having previously been totally devoid of awareness. In other words, for these 'deniers' awareness of existence doesn't exist; all that exists is a delusional dream. This position is surely unacceptable. A world exists and awareness of the existence of this existing world exists. Awareness is aware that when it doesn't exist often dreams exist.

What does it mean to say that experience exists? It is certain that experience exists because awareness is aware that experience exists. Awareness is aware of a whole range of experiences – the tingling sensation in the foot, the sight of a tree, the ache in the tooth, the chirping of a bird, the smell of burnt toast, the taste of ginger, the touch of velvet, the thought: "this is velvet:", being punched in the head, the feeling of elation, and the burning sensation on the skin. These things are all experiences which awareness is aware of.

What does it mean to say that qualia exist? To say that qualia exist is simply to say that awareness is aware that raw feels or phenomenological qualities exist. The experience of having a burning sensation on the skin has a certain raw feel – a qualitative phenomenology of what-it-is-like to be undergoing that particular experience. It is certain that qualia exist because awareness is aware that raw feels exist.

Task 2 – Elucidating possible relations between the phenomena

It is certain that experience and qualia exist because awareness exists and awareness is aware that experience and qualia exist. What is not certain is how the three phenomena are related.

One possibility is that both experience and qualia could exist in the absence of awareness. In other words when awareness temporarily vanishes experience and qualia continue to exist; furthermore, experience and qualia could have existed before the foundations for awareness were in place. An alternative possibility is that both experience and qualia are dependent on the existence of awareness for their existence. In other words the question is: Does the emergence of awareness bring with it the simultaneous emergence of experience and qualia, or does the emergence of awareness entail awareness of pre-existing experience and qualia?

To say that the emergence of awareness entails awareness of pre-existing experience and qualia is to say that experience and qualia existed in the universe before awareness did. Indeed, it would be experiential interactions which created the foundations for awareness to emerge from inexistence. In this possible relation between the phenomena awareness is aware of experiences and qualia but is itself wholly devoid of these properties. It would be inappropriate to call awareness an experiencer – awareness is awareness of experiencers. It would only make sense to refer to awareness as an experiencer if the emergence of awareness brought with it the simultaneous emergence of experience and qualia.

When it comes to the relation between experience and qualia it is possible that some experiences entail qualia whilst other experiences do not. Alternatively, it is possible that all experiences entail qualia. What is not possible is for qualia to exist without experience – the existence of qualia necessarily entails the existence of experience. The most likely possibility is that some experiences entail qualia whilst some experiences do not entail qualia. There is a raw feel associated with being punched in the head, but not with seeing a piece of paper. Both events are experiences but only the former has a raw feel.

The possibility that some experiences are devoid of qualia means that there are two sets of possible relations which need to be elucidated – those between experience and awareness, and those between qualia and awareness. Regarding the second of these relations, it is possible that awareness is aware of an experience but that there are no qualia in awareness. Regarding the first relation, the question is whether awareness can exist without being aware of any experiences. It is surely the case that expertise in meditation can lead to a vast decrease in the experiences that awareness is aware of at a particular moment. However, it is also surely the case that awareness has to be aware of at least one experience. If awareness wasn't aware of anything then it wouldn't be awareness. For awareness to exist there has to be an experience which awareness is aware of. An experience vacuum would send awareness back to the realm of inexistence. Awareness could possibly exist without qualia, but not without experience.

Task 3 – Is it possible to know how the phenomena actually relate to each other?

Awareness can only know about what it is aware of – it cannot know of what it is unaware. Awareness cannot know if any other awareness exists. Awareness cannot know whether all the universe that it is not has experience and qualia. Awareness cannot know whether that which preceded its emergence was itself experiencing and qualing. A defining feature of awareness is lack of awareness.

Awareness is aware of a vast array of experiences – these are its domain. It is surely possible that awareness can become aware of which of these experiences have qualia. Awareness could become aware that simple physical interactions entail experiential qualia, whilst the operations of functional structures result in experiences without qualia. In other words, the thought generated by the operations of the brain, the vision generated by the eye, and the hearing generated by the ear, could all be experiences without qualia. Whilst, simple physical interactions such as touching velvet, being punched in the head, smelling burnt toast, and a knife cutting a finger, are all experiences which entail qualia. This knowledge is surely possible.

Knowledge of the pervasiveness and longevity of experience and qualia is something of which awareness is terminally unaware. This knowledge is not possible for it is outside of the scope of what awareness can become aware of.

Task 4 - Assessing the arguments for possible relations between the phenomena

The exact nature of the relation between awareness on the one hand, and experience and qualia on the other, is the relation which awareness cannot know; this relation can only be approached through assessing the merits of the arguments for the possible relations. There are two possible relations which will be considered:

PR1:   The emergence of awareness is also the emergence of experience and qualia.

PR2:   When awareness emerges it becomes aware of pre-existing experience and qualia.

There are three further possibilities which will not be considered. It has been claimed that all of these positions are either incoherent or highly implausible:

PR3:   Awareness does not emerge – the entire universe is aware.

PR4:   Awareness exists first and at a later time experience and qualia emerge.

PR5:   Awareness does not exist – everything is a lifelong delusional dream.

What are the arguments for PR1 and PR2? The most obvious argument in support of PR2 is the

implausibility of PR1. To hold that all of the phenomena emerged and that they all emerged at
exactly the same time is quite a stretch of the
imagination. Many would go so far as to argue that
the notion of the emergence of the experiential from
the wholly non-experiential, and the emergence of
qualia from the wholly non-qualia, is blatantly
incoherent. The idea is that whilst it is sensible to
talk about things such as the emergence of the living
from the non-living, it isn't even sensible to suggest
that something wholly devoid of experience and
qualia could give rise to these phenomena.

What arguments are there in support of PR1?
The most obvious argument seems to be that the
parts of the universe which appear to be unaware
show no signs of having experience and qualia. The
problem with this argument is that experience and
qualia are not things which publically reveal themselves; they are phenomena which are directly
experienced and felt by awareness. Where there is
no awareness there will be no knowledge of experience and qualia. This means that the supporter of
PR1 has to simply assert: "PR2 seems implausible".
And, of course, the supporter of PR2 can respond
that PR1 seems even more implausible.

The supporter of PR2 could try and convince his opponent by giving an evolutionary story such as the following: *The origin of life requires that the universe is exceptionally finely-tuned, life has evolved into highly complex organisms, and the non-aware has arranged itself in such a way as to provide the foundations for awareness. Why not accept that these outcomes are the result of qualia involving experiential interactions – interactions that have order and consistency due to the presence of experience and qualia? This seems to be more plausible than these outcomes arising from wholly non-experiential stuff bashing into itself.*

The supporter of PR1 will assert that there is no need for such a fanciful story as there are laws of physics which give order to the evolution of the universe. The supporter of PR2 asks for evidence of these laws and asserts that what we call 'laws' are 'consistency relationships' which evolved over a long period of time through a plethora of experiential interactions. The supporter of PR1 asserts that laws are eternal and unchanging but also acknowledges ignorance of exactly what was happening ten billion years ago.

So, we have two possible relations. The fact that awareness cannot know if what it is unaware of exists means that various arguments need to be advanced as to the likelihood as to whether or not awareness becomes aware of pre-existing experiences and qualia. It is possible that the supporter of PR2 has the more convincing arguments. The supporter of PR1 is forced to admit the emergence of more phenomena, to account for their simultaneous emergence, and his main response is simply: "that seems implausible". This response by itself is clearly inadequate as many things which seem implausible are true. Of course, this also means that however implausible or incoherent PR3, PR4 and PR5 seem to be they cannot be totally discounted themselves.

Let us look briefly at the implications of PR2. If this position is correct it is likely that awareness itself does not do anything; it is simply an epiphenomenal observer of its engulfing surroundings – the 'body-world'. In this scenario the fundamental distinction in reality is not between mind (i.e. rational thought) and body, or mind and matter, or mind and world, or even living and non-living; it is between the aware and the unaware.

Reflection 2

Hearing

When I hear certain sounds I am 'grated' – I feel really uncomfortable; an example of such a sound is that produced when fingernails scratch a blackboard.[3] When I hear other sounds I am 'chimed' – my spirits are lifted; an example of such a sound is the chirping of birds. Why is this? Why do certain sounds 'grate' me and others 'chime' with me?

In what follows I reflect on this question. The first step is to divide the question into two premises:

P1   I have the ability to hear sounds because I possess ears (most parts of reality are unable to hear sounds).

P2   When I hear certain sounds I am 'grated', when I hear other sounds I am 'chimed'.

---

[3] The phrases 'I' and 'me' refer to the awareness of existence that is writing these words.

I am happy to assume that the reason I can hear a sound when fingernails scratch a blackboard is that I possess ears, which means that most of reality – which is very un-earlike – cannot hear a sound when fingernails scratch a blackboard. Furthermore, I am certain that this particular sound causes me to be 'grated' because every time I hear fingernails scratching a blackboard I become aware of a shiver down my spine, sickness in my stomach, and start to tense up; it is surely the fingernail scratching that is causing this 'grating'.

The main question is: Is P2 dependent on P1? In other words: Does the hearing of a sound itself contain the 'grating' and the 'chiming'? Or, are there two distinct things occurring. Firstly, a particular vibration of air molecules which emanates from a specific location and which either 'chimes' or 'grates' with the surroundings that it encounters as it ripples through space-time. Secondly, the conversion of the vibration into sounds when it encounters an ear?

I take it that the overwhelmingly dominant view is that P2 is dependent on P1. In fact, as far as I am aware, the possibility that 'there are two distinct things going on' has not been seriously considered before (but it surely has). I will be arguing for the possibility that there are two utterly distinct things going on – hearing sounds on the one hand, and 'grating'/'chiming' on the other.

I am not suggesting that as the vibrations radiate out from the scratched blackboard most of the surroundings are aware that they are being 'grated' or 'chimed'. On this view, the 'grating' and 'chiming' is obliviously occurring in most of reality. It is only in a few parts of reality that there is awareness of the 'grating' and 'chiming'. Of course, if this is correct, it suggests an entire 'world view' in which vibrations are central. All of reality is vibrating in resonance with the rest of reality. As a person speaks vibrations radiate out from their voice-box and will 'chime' with particular surroundings and 'grate' with others. As the tone of their voice is changed those surroundings which were previously 'chimed' can become 'grated'. It is not the particular spoken words which are important, but the manner of their projection. It is perhaps the case that a caring and soothing voice is more likely to 'chime' with its surroundings, whilst a spiteful and sarcastic voice is more likely to 'grate' with its surroundings. However, the same voice can both 'grate' some surroundings and 'chime' with others.

It is possible that some may find such a possibility too absurd to warrant consideration. However, it really is not absurd. It is well known that when contact is made with one's body either a 'chiming' or a 'grating' effect results. There is a mass of evidence that simply being touched on the skin in an affectionate way results in a lifting of the spirits, a sense of well-being – a 'chiming effect'. Whilst, when the skin comes into contact with some objects – such as a snake skin, for example – a repulsive 'grating effect' often results. Furthermore, when the body interacts with rays from the Sun a 'chiming effect' usually results – a sense of warmth and happiness. Given all of this, it should be expected that when vibrating air molecules interact with our body that either a 'chiming' or a 'grating' effect will result. If there is resonance between the particular vibrations in our body and the vibrating air molecules at the moment they interact then there will be 'chiming' – otherwise there will be 'grating'.

Of course, it should be obvious that gathering empirical support for the position defended here is possible. If a deaf person is repeatedly 'grated' by a fingernail scratching a blackboard, then the 'grating' is surely utterly distinct from hearing. Of course, the deaf person may be utterly oblivious to the fact that when they feel a certain way this is because finger-nails are scratching a blackboard. In fact, there is already evidence that "the functionally deaf patient may orient to ambient sounds"[4]. Of course, from the perspective argued for here it would be more accurate to say: "the functionally deaf patient may orient to, and be 'chimed'/'grated' by, vibrating air molecules; he is unaware of sounds". To say that "certain sounds grate me" is really to say "certain vibrations of air molecules grate me".

One might be convinced that there is a simpler explanation as to why certain sounds 'grate' and others 'chime'; an explanation that is bound up with the hearing of the sound itself. A simple account could be given in which the blood-curdling scream 'grates' me because I immediately know that some-one is in great pain or trouble, and I feel bad for them, and possibly scared myself. This could be expanded into an evolutionary account in which 'chiming' and 'grating' have an explanation through

---

[4] Kilhstrom, J., Barnhardt, T., Tartaryn, D., "Implicit Perception", in Bornstein and Pittman (eds.), *Perception Without Awareness*, (Guilford Press: London, 1992) p. 29.

evolutionary psychology. So, the reason why the blood-curdling scream 'grates' me would be that when the human brain was developing such screams were inevitably associated with bad things – such as being attacked by predators – which necessitated a 'flight or fight' response which was motivated by a 'grating' feeling. In other words, those humans who were 'grated' by screams and reacted accordingly survived and this 'screaming-grating' association became propagated through evolution.

This evolutionary psychology account could explain why some sounds 'grate' me and others 'chime' with me. In doing so it appears to support the position that P2 is dependent on P1. However, this account gives no explanation of the existence of 'grating' and 'chiming' in the first place. It simply explains why those early humans who were 'chimed' by the sound of a blood curdling scream were not favoured in the evolutionary process, whereas those who were 'grated' by the sound were favoured. The thing in need of explanation is why 'grating' or 'chiming' is related to sound in the first place.

Another problem for the evolutionary account is that a plethora of sounds cause me to become aware of being 'grated' or 'chimed', and the majority of these seem to be unsuited to such an evolutionary explanation. It is hard to imagine an evolutionary account of why I am 'chimed' by particular pieces of classical music and 'grated' when I hear an automobile engine. The more plausible explanation is surely that I am not being 'grated' or 'chimed' by the sound which is created by my ears, but that my entire body is 'grated' and 'chimed' by particular frequencies and patterns of vibrations of air molecules. This explanation simply entails there being a spectrum of vibration patterns – some of these 'chime' with my body and some 'grate' my body. It is irrelevant what is causing the particular vibration pattern; it is simply a brute fact that some frequencies and patterns 'grate' whilst others 'chime'. So, the reason I am 'grated' by a piece of rap music, an automobile engine, fingernails scratching a blackboard, and a blood curdling scream, is that they all have similarities in their vibrations – similarities which cause them to 'grate' with my body. Conversely, there is another family of vibrations – which includes chirping birds and particular pieces of classical music – which 'chimes' with my body.

The extraordinary ability of music to 'chime' and 'grate' is well known. Long ago Aristotle pondered: "How is it that rhythms and melodies, although only sound, resemble states of the soul?"[5] Whilst, Schopenhauer claimed that: "[Music] gives the innermost kernel preceding all form, or the heart of things"[6]. If one accepts that P2 is dependent on P1 then these claims are fairly unfathomable. However, if it is accepted that P2 isn't dependent on P1 – that all vibrations of air molecules 'chime' or 'grate' with their surroundings – then we get a particular insight into these statements. We can see that rhythms and melodies are not "only sound" which is created by ears – they are also particular patterns of vibrations of air molecules which either 'chime' or 'grate' with the surroundings they encounter and thereby directly affect the entire human body. It is this interaction which causes rhythms and melodies to "resemble states of the soul". As these vibration patterns interact with every atom in the body there

───────────────────

[5] Aristotle, cited in Schopenhauer, Arthur, *The World as Will and Representation*, Volume I, Trans. E. F. J. Payne, (New York: Dover Publications, 1969), p. 260.

[6] Schopenhauer, Arthur, *The World as Will and Representation*, Volume I, Trans. E. F. J. Payne, (New York: Dover Publications, 1969), p. 263.

is also a real sense in which music is at "the heart of things", and in which interactions between atoms – interactions which entail particular vibration patterns – are the "innermost kernel" which precedes all form.

Reflection 3

Memory

Let us reflect on the phenomenon of memory. Memories exist of experiences that occurred in the past. Some humans have very good memories and some humans have very bad memories. At one extreme are humans who have absolutely no memory of most of their life due to a rare brain condition, whilst at the other extreme are rare savants who can immediately recall every minor event in their entire life.

There are many interesting memory phenomena. There is the phenomenon of implicit memory where humans cannot recall things if asked, but these things are stored in memory and influence their future behaviour. There are curious cases where humans cannot recall what they were doing when hypnotised unless they are re-hypnotised and questioned about what they were doing when they were hypnotised the first time. There is the widespread phenomenon, which surely everyone has regularly experienced, wherein one tries in vain to remember something but is sure that it is 'on the tip-of-the-tongue' – stored somewhere but temporarily inaccessible. And of course, many will have experienced the phenomenon of being drunk and not even being able to recall one's name or address. Furthermore, access to memory seems so much easier when one is full of energy and alert, compared to when one is tired. Finally, old age seems to bring with it an increasing propensity for deteriorating memory in the majority of humans.

The question is: "Why does the capacity to recall memories vary so much?" It is very tempting to believe that the memories of the drunk, the aged, the tip-of-the-tongued, and the brain-conditioned, still exist. Surely, when the drunk sobers up he will remember his name, that which was on the tip-of-the-tongue will be recalled, the human with the rare brain-condition could possibly recover the memories of their past life in the future, and the memories of the elderly are still potentially recoverable if the right stimulus to memory recall presents itself. If this is right, then the differences in memory recall capacity are largely or wholly due to a lack of access to memories rather than to a difference in the storage of memories. The major 'memory difference' between humans would be the ability to recall memories rather than the ability to store memories. There undoubtedly are large differences between humans in their ability to recall memories. The question is: Are there any differences between humans in their ability to store memories?

There are three possibilities if an experience cannot be recalled. The experience wasn't stored as a memory in the first place, it is stored but cannot be accessed, or it was stored but was later erased. To decide between these possibilities requires addressing the issue of how experiences come to be stored as memories. Are all experiences stored? Are memories things which can be erased? Or, are memories things which exist forever but often cannot be accessed?

The role of the brain is clearly of central importance in any attempt to answer these questions. What role does the brain play in memory? I am happy to assume that memories are stored in the brain. Furthermore, it is surely the case that the brain plays a role in the access to memories. A question that needs to be asked is: Are memories stored in things other than brains? It is possible that memories are stored in the fundamental constitu-ents of reality – the very fabric of the universe itself. If this is the case, then the storage capacity of memories in all humans would be identical. The brain itself would be an organ which enables access to memories rather than providing unique storage of them. Differences in brains would explain the differences in access ability between humans. Whilst the current state of particular brains would explain transitory variations in access ability such as that experienced by the drunk and the 'tip-of-the-tongued'.

Is there any evidence for such a position? There are, in fact, five main areas of evidence which provide support for the claim that memories are more widespread than brains. Firstly, memory transfer in organ transplantation. Secondly, the phenomenon of the 'medium'. Thirdly, memories of previous lives. Fourthly, homeopathy. Finally, the memory in quanta conclusively established by quantum mechanics. Let us take each of these in turn.

The first area of evidence is memory transfer in organ transplantation. The most striking evidence comes from heart transplants where following transplantation the recipient inherits the preferences of the donor. Pearsall *et al* (2002) in investigating this phenomenon found that: "Two to 5 parallels per case were observed between changes following surgery and the histories of the donors. Parallels included changes in food, music, art, sexual, recreational, and career preferences, as well as specific instances of perceptions of names and sensory experiences related to the donors."[7]

The most likely explanation for this phenomenon is that memories are transferred from donor to recipient. So, when the donor is a lover of classical music and has a plethora of joyous memories listening to it, the recipient inherits these memories. This causes the previously classical music hating recipient to suddenly start loving classical music. In one case the recipients wife is utterly bewildered when her husband starts reciting classical songs and listening to classical music incessantly following the transplant. The recipient claims: "I used to hate

---

[7] Pearsall, Paul, Schwartz, Gary E. R., Russek, Linda G. S., "Changes in Heart Transplant Recipients That Parallel the Personalities of Their Donors", *Journal of Near-Death Studies*, 20 (3), Spring 2002, p. 191.

classical music, but now I love it. So I know it's not my new heart, because a black guy from the 'hood wouldn't be into that. Now it calms my heart. I play it all the time."[8] Of course, the recipient actually did love classical music and was shot on the way to his violin class. The recipient's wife claims: "He's driving me nuts with the classical music. He doesn't know the name of one song and never, never listened to it before. Now, he sits for hours and listens to it."[9]

Let us not ignore the knowledge we have of this phenomenon but rather seek an explanation for it. It is obviously the case that memories affect behaviour, and emotion-laden memories will have a particularly strong affect on future preferences and action. Joyous memories of listening to classical music can obviously play a role in motivating one to listen to

[8] Pearsall, Paul, Schwartz, Gary E. R., Russek, Linda G. S., "Changes in Heart Transplant Recipients That Parallel the Personalities of Their Donors", *Journal of Near-Death Studies*, 20 (3), Spring 2002, p. 197.

[9] Pearsall, Paul, Schwartz, Gary E. R., Russek, Linda G. S., "Changes in Heart Transplant Recipients That Parallel the Personalities of Their Donors", *Journal of Near-Death Studies*, 20 (3), Spring 2002, pp. 197-8.

classical music. It is utterly irrelevant whether the memories were generated by the experiences of another human.

We here have evidence that memories are stored not in brains but in parts of the body of a human. If memories are stored in the organs that are transplanted into donors, then we have to wonder whether memories are stored in every single part of the body. It is surely highly probable that this is in fact the case. Memories are stored in all body parts, whilst we only get to know of this phenomenon because a very tiny fraction of body parts end up transplanted into another human. It is only in these cases that the effects of the memories reveal themselves through the experiences and actions of the recipient. In these cases the changes in the recipient are so striking that the phenomenon of stored memory starkly reveals itself.

Can humans become aware of the memories that are stored in body parts that are not part of their own body? This is an interesting question. Let us reflect on this possibility. In particular let us reflect on those humans who genuinely believe themselves to be 'spiritual mediums'. These 'mediums' believe they are in contact with the souls of the deceased. Some also show a seemingly remarkable ability to touch the surroundings which engulfed a deceased human (such as their clothes) and thereby access the memories of the deceased with amazing accuracy. Let us not ignore the knowledge of this possibility but rather accept that memories could possibly exist in all of the surroundings which engulf humans, not just in body parts. I wouldn't like to claim that there are no such things as 'human immortal souls', but it is surely possible that the 'medium' is actually in contact with memories stored in the surroundings engulfing humans, rather than with an 'immortal soul'.

In other words, the 'medium' can be considered to be a 'point of access' to memories which are stored in both humans and all of their surroundings. The term 'point of access' means exactly the same thing as the term 'awareness' which was used in *Reflection One*. The 'medium' has privileged access because their access point is 'unclouded'. Let us consider the gift of the 'medium' to be our second area of evidence for the pervasiveness of memories in the surroundings which engulf humans.

This takes us nicely into our third area of evidence which is the vast number of cases in which infants provide detailed memories of the experiences of people who have lived in the past. There is surely a good reason why this phenomenon usually occurs in infants. The 'point of access' to memories that are stored in both humans and their surroundings that arises in an infant is also 'unclouded' – it is free from the baggage of experiences that have been generated by the life of an older human. The infant is both 'pure' and 'selfless' (perhaps like our 'medium'). There is a plethora of evidence for this phenomena but the standard assumption is that an 'immortal human soul' exists which both inhabited the body that had the past experiences and now inhabits the body of the human recalling those experiences. This idea of the 'immortal human soul' is now highly unpopular and is considered to be 'unscientific'. The result of this is that the evidence for the phenomena is largely ignored. Perhaps many would find the proposal that memories are stored in the very fabric of the universe itself more appealing. No doubt many would prefer to ignore the knowledge of the phenomenon altogether.

The fourth area of evidence is provided by homeopathy. Homeopathic cures are dependent on memory because the active ingredient is diluted to such a degree that none of it is left in the remedy. All that is left is the memory of the active ingredient. The effectiveness of homeopathic cures is hard to judge because of other possibilities affecting the human such as the 'placebo effect'. However, if the evidence for homeopathic remedies increases then this would provide strong support for the pervasiveness of memory in the surroundings which engulf humans.

The fifth area of evidence comes from quantum mechanics. Repeated experiments have shown that when entangled photons are fired great distances apart they retain a memory of the existence of their counterpart. When one photon shifts into an 'up' state the other automatically shifts into a 'down' state. This is strong 'scientific' evidence for memory in the very fabric of the surroundings which engulf humans.

Bringing these areas together gives rise to the following possibility. If humans and all of their surroundings have evolved from the Big Bang then they will be an entangled web of differential memory relationships. In other words, every experience that has ever existed since the beginning of the universe would be stored in all parts of the surroundings

which engulf humans. Experiences that are generated in a particular place and time will be more
easily available to a 'point of access' located in that
time and place than more distantly (both spatially
and temporally) generated experiences will be.
However, at some level all experiences are stored
and are potentially accessible to any 'point of access'.
More distant experiences are more likely to come to
prominence in dreams, when one is hypnotised, or
when one is very young.

Reflection 4

The Perception of Objects

Let us consider the relationship between the perceiver of an object and an object. Is it not an obvious truth that an object can only exist when it is perceived as an object? On hearing such a claim it is easy to respond: "Surely the horse still exists in the stable when I am in my office, and the chair still exists in my office when I am in the stable. Therefore, the objects 'chair' and 'horse' exist when they are unperceived". However, this response is clearly hopelessly inadequate. It comes a stage too late and glosses over the preliminary question of what it means for a 'chair' and a 'horse' to exist for a perceiver in the first place. Clearly, if a chair exists for me when I am in my office, then when I am in the stable the chair will, in normal circumstances, still exist for me if I return to the office. However, the chair wouldn't exist as an 'object' in the first place unless I perceive it as such. When I am in the stable there is no perception-independent object called a 'chair' in the office, there is only an arrangement of stuff that is a 'chair' if it is directly perceived as a chair. Similarly, when I am in the office all that exists in the stable is an arrangement of stuff that if directly perceived by me will be a 'horse'. It is perfectly coherent to assert: "If I was in the stable at this very moment I would perceive a horse, but as I am in my office at this very moment there is no horse in the stable."

It is easy to believe that the issue at stake is which objects would exist for me if I was somewhere else. But this is not the case. The issue is simply: "What is it for any object to exist for me?" Clearly, it is obviously true that no objects exist for me unless I am observing them at this very moment. If I am not directly observing an object then it doesn't exist as an object for me. If there is no object for me then there is no sense in the notion that there is an object. Of course, I can think about objects that I might encounter if I turned around or entered another room, but this thinking about objects is far removed from the actual existence of objects. I can think: "If I turn around I will perceive a table" and if I have perceived a table behind me a few seconds before then it is very likely that I will be correct. However, I can also think: "If I turn around I will perceive a mermaid riding a unicorn". In this case it is very likely that I will not be correct. Thoughts about the possible existence of objects relate to possibilities not actualities.

It is perfectly acceptable to engage in speculation about the possible existence of objects – "If I was in Paris I would perceive the Eiffel Tower". However, this is clearly just speculation. It says nothing more than – "If I was at Loch Ness I might perceive the Loch Ness Monster." One might object that the Eiffel Tower actually exists as an object, whilst the Loch Ness Monster doesn't; the Eiffel Tower exists even if I am not perceiving it. However, this is obviously wrong. One only need think of the period after the eleventh September 2001 and all those deluded humans who were convinced that the Twin Towers exist in New York – that if they went there they would perceive them. If I am talking on the phone to a friend who claims: "the Eiffel Tower exists – I can perceive it now" then presuming that they are not mistaken I know that this object exists for them, and that if I was in Paris at that very moment it would surely exist for me too.

Similarly, one may be tempted to assert that they know that a 'cat' exists in the room next door because they can hear a 'meowing' sound and a voice saying: "Don't worry moggy it is time for your bowl of milk!" However, when they go to the room there is no 'cat' – just a playing tape recorder. Anyone who claims that unperceived objects exist is simply speculating about the various possibilities that the universe contains to present different objects to them.

Let us assume that a human has been moulded by a process of evolution – both over the time period of the evolution of the human species, and the time period of the evolution of an individual organism. This means that the objects that are perceived by a human – and which can thereafter enter 'awareness' – will be dependent on this particular evolutionary process. The objects perceived by a human are created by that human. To say that a human 'creates' objects does not mean that when they are aware of a 'tree' that nothing exists where the tree exists. It simply means that this stuff would not be a distinct object without being isolated by a human as such. A perceiver is a 'delineator' – a 'carver up' of its engulfing surroundings. Of course, every perceiver will 'carve up' reality in a unique way. Humans that have been moulded by a very similar process of evolution – both over the time period of the evolution of the human species, and the time period of the evolution of an individual human – will 'carve up' reality in a very similar way. Whilst humans that have been moulded by a very different evolutionary process will 'carve up' reality in a very different way.

One important point to make explicit is that 'object creation' and 'awareness of objects' are two distinct things. Awareness cannot be aware of an object unless a human creates the object, but the human perceptual apparatus continuously creates objects which awareness is not aware of. This is a crucial point and means that objects can be perceived without awareness. It follows that parts of reality could create objects without there ever being any awareness that objects are being created in that area of space-time. A normal human is usually aware of some of the objects that their perceptual apparatus is creating because a normal human is a part of reality that has awareness. What about non-human animals? It is surely possible that some species of non-human animals have sets of perceptual apparatus which create objects, but don't have any awareness that this is going on. That is to say 'reality is being carved up' but there is no awareness of the existence of either objects or reality.

For human and non-human animals it seems that the simpler the perceptual apparatus the simpler will be the 'carving'. If one struggles to conceptualise this one needs to reflect upon the difference between a painting created by a typical five year old child and a painting created by a great artist such as Picasso.

So, every perceptual apparatus creates objects. More complex sets of perceptual apparatus create more objects. Reality is one, but it can be carved up in an immense number of ways. In at least one animal there is awareness of objects, but an animal can create objects without having the awareness that these objects exist. Some animals surely create objects, and react to those objects, without awareness of those objects.

What does all this mean in concrete terms? It means that when I observe my lounge I see a plethora of objects – the television which I know will show various programmes if I turn it on, the television remote control which is placed on the sofa, the batteries which are showing because the back of the remote is removed, the springs which hold the batteries in place within the remote, the table, the tablecloth, the candles, the candleholder, the coasters, the books, the CDs, the DVDs, the plant, and the plantpot. All of these things exist for me because of the evolutionary process – both over the time period of the evolution of the human species and the time period of the evolution of me – that my brain has gone through. These things will also exist for parts of reality that have gone through a similar evolutionary process to my brain. They will clearly not exist for parts of reality which have gone through a very different evolutionary process. A 'coaster' and a 'DVD' will not exist as objects for a rat, or for a cat. This isn't to say that a rat, or a cat, couldn't isolate the area of space-time that a human labels 'DVD'. It is possible that they could distinguish this area from its surroundings, although it is also possible that they could not. The important point is that this area won't be delineated from its surroundings as a distinct 'object'.

The perception-dependentness of life

One might be comfortable with the claim that a 'DVD' doesn't exist as a distinct object for a cat. However, it might be claimed, surely the cat itself exists as a distinct object even if I am not observing it. Furthermore, surely other humans exist as distinct objects even if I am not observing them. It might even be claimed to be nonsensical to deny these things. Nevertheless, let us deny these things; they are incompatible with the 'obvious truth' that an object can only exist if it is perceived as such. I wish to defend the assertion that horses, humans, and cats, do not exist as such unless I perceive them as such. I can perceive a human or a cat at a particular location, but when this location is unperceived there is no delineated object existing at this location.

However, this is not the complete picture. Whilst objects only exist for the perceivers that perceive them as such, there is more to reality than the perceivable. The perceptual apparatus of a human moulds the perceivable part of reality into objects which can exist in awareness. The unperceivable exists irrespective of whether or not it is perceived. Part of the unperceivable part of reality is

55

the awareness of reality which arises in certain parts of reality. So, if awareness exists in particular humans, horses, and cats, then this awareness will exist irrespective of whether a perceiver perceives 'humans', 'horses' and 'cats'.

The perceivable part of reality when it is unperceived is utterly undifferentiated. This means that this part of reality is simply a set of movements – a massive array of different movements. Nothing is at rest – everything moves. Of course, when a certain pattern of movements occurs in a particular part of reality – i.e. the perceptual apparatus of a 'human' – then the result is that these movements mould the undifferentiated into differentiable objects. In other words, certain sets of movements within the undifferentiated have the capacity to mould other movements within the undifferentiated into objects. When I become aware of a 'living entity' my perceptual apparatus has 'carved up' the undifferentiated by isolating a particular set of movements. 'Living entities' are parts of the undifferentiated which exhibit those movements we call 'metabolising movements'. The simplistic carving of the undifferentiated into 'life' versus 'non-life' is perception dependent.

A further elucidation of these points may be useful. The basic point is that the awareness that exists in a human will be located in part of their brain – not one specific part, but as something generated by the movements of various parts, and which is therefore located where those various parts are located. Some parts can flit into and out of awareness – the 'area of awareness' itself moves. When I perceive a human I cannot perceive their awareness. I do not perceive this differentiable part of reality as an object. Rather, I mould the undifferentiated into an object which comprises arms, legs, and a head, etc., and observe this whole as an 'object'. When unperceived all that exists is the undifferentiated stuff of the universe, which is a set of diverse movements, and differentiable, but unperceivable, bits of moving awareness. Certain movements in the undifferentiated have the capacity to mould other movements into objects. This 'object formation' can exist without awareness, but sometimes accompanies awareness. This means that all living entities only exist as differentiated objects when they are perceived as such.

One might object that to say that all that exists when a particular perceiver does not perceive the world is differentiable but unperceivable awareness on the one hand, and undifferentiated stuff which is differentiated into objects through perception on the other, is obviously false. Surely, the objection goes, living organisms *as a whole* exist as differentiated stuff independently of being perceived as differentiated. The position which has been outlined here denies this and asserts that all of an organism except its unperceivable awareness is undifferentiated. However, it is accepted that it is very easy to fall into the trap of believing that there is such a thing as a differentiated entity which a human might perceive and call a 'cat' which exists as a differentiated whole independent of this perceiving. In order to avail oneself of this trap it is perhaps useful to first comprehend that there is no such thing as perception-independent 'species' of animals/living things. If this is fully comprehended then it becomes much easier to understand how there is no such thing as a perception-independent animal.

The perception-dependentness of species

Let us recap. We have seen that the part of the undifferentiated that metabolises we call 'living', whilst the part of the undifferentiated that doesn't metabolise we call the 'non-living'. The 'living' and the 'non-living' are simply different parts of the undifferentiated. Metabolism doesn't produce differentiation, only a particular kind of movement. Both the 'living' and the 'non-living' move. Movement is a fundamental characteristic of the undifferentiated and has nothing to do with differentiation. The distinction between 'living' and 'non-living' requires a perceiver who perceives particular kinds of movements and segregates them into two kinds – the 'metabolising' kind and the 'non-metabolising' kind. There are a multitude of other segregations of movements in the undifferentiated which could be made. Nevertheless, the distinction between 'metabolising movements' and 'non-metabolising movements' is a real and interesting distinction within the observable undifferentiated.

What could it possibly mean to assert that the 'living' – which is itself simply part of the undifferentiated – could itself be differentiated into a plethora of 'species'? The most common definition of a 'species' asserts that any metabolising entities which can produce metabolising entities which can themselves produce metabolising entities are members of a 'species'. The fact that there other definitions of a 'species' should immediately set the alarm bells ringing about the possible vacuousness of the concept. However, let us focus on the most common definition.

According to this definition 'species' of 'cats', 'dogs' and 'ladybirds', etc., have a perception-independent existence which is delineated by their ability to produce fertile offspring. However, there is evidence that sometimes two members of radically different 'species' – even from different classes and phyla – can interact and produce fertile offspring. Donald Williamson asserts that: "Such successful matings between very distantly related animals occurred infrequently, some thirty to fifty times in 541 million years. This means a fertile, successful outcome happens roughly once in 10 million years."[10] These infrequent occurrences clearly undermine the common definition of a 'species' because the implication is that members of different classes of 'species' both are different 'species' and the same 'species' at the same time.

---

[10] Williamson, Donald, cited in Margulis, Lynn, and Sagan, Dorion, *Acquiring Genomes: A theory of the origins of species*, (New York: Basic Books, 2002), p. 166.

There are surely no sharp delineations between 'species'. It is simply the case that when parts of the metabolising undifferentiated which have a lot of similarities interact there is a high chance of fertile offspring, whilst when parts of the metabolising undifferentiated which have very few similarities interact there is a low chance of fertile offspring. We are talking about probabilities, not sharp delineations, in the metabolising undifferentiated.

One might object that a perceiver can directly perceive different 'species' for themselves simply through perception of the visual similarities of different parts of the metabolising undifferentiated. Of course, such an objection quickly results in absurdity. Simply consider the close similarity between a 'horse' and a 'donkey', and the vast difference between a 'white-skinned midget male human' and a 'dark-skinned giant female human'. Clearly, visual appearance would suggest that the former pair are more likely to be members of the same 'species' than the latter pair.

The only acceptable conclusion is that 'species' are purely perception-dependent creations. Acceptance of the conclusion that there is no such thing as a perception-independent species can help one understand how there is no such thing as a perception-independent animal. All that exists in the domain of the perceptionless is differentiable but unobservable awareness and undifferentiated stuff. Within the undifferentiated a perceiver can isolate certain movements of stuff and call these movements (metabolism) the 'living', he can then attempt to segregate these movements into distinct perception-independent 'species' but he is doomed to fail, the divisions are wholly arbitrary and perception-dependent. The perception-dependentness of 'species' is a stage above the delineation of particular animals. A species-less animal is simply a set of utterly unique movements within the undifferentiated.

So, one might believe that a perception-independent metabolising entity called a 'seagull' exists, and that there is a whole 'species' of 'seagulls'. In reality, when a perceiver perceives a single 'seagull' flying in the sky, all that he is perceiving and isolating is a particular set of movements within the observable undifferentiated. When a perceiver perceives a 'flock of seagulls', all that he is perceiving and isolating are several similar but unique sets of movements within the observable undifferentiated.

The particular sets of movements that are isolated depend on the make-up of the perceiver. There are no unperceived objects.

One final thing to reflect upon is the pervasiveness of 'object creation'. 'Object awareness' is obviously constrained to those parts of the undifferentiated that have awareness. However, we have seen that other parts of the undifferentiated (simple 'species' of non-human animals) could quite feasibly 'create objects' without 'object awareness'. We have, so far, limited our focus to 'object creation' by animals. But animals are just particular patterns of movements within the undifferentiated. So, it has to be possible that non-animal movement patterns could also be engaged in 'object creation'. In fact it has to be possible that every movement in the undifferentiated entails 'object creation'. If we look at a simple movement such as two 'atoms' moving towards each other to form a 'molecule' then it is surely possible that each atom, through its 'internal' movements, creates the 'object' that is the other 'atom'. However, this is a very different thing from 'object awareness'.

Returning to *Reflection One*, it should also be noted that the division made here between the 'observable undifferentiated' and 'differentiable but unperceivable awareness' is too simplistic. We saw there that there are good reasons to believe that all of the 'observable undifferentiated' may itself contain a largely unperceivable side – the realm of experience and qualia. This means that we don't simply have the 'observable undifferentiated' and 'differentiable but unperceivable awareness', we also have the 'experiential undifferentiated which is both perceivable and unperceivable'. In other words, experiences and raw feels intermingle throughout the undifferentiated and some of these enter a particular awareness.

Reflection 5

Thought and Freedom

What is it to have a thought? Is thought related to freedom? How pervasive in the universe is thought? These seem to be the most pertinent questions relating to the notion of thought. Thinking is a familiar phenomenon; familiar but mysterious. Most people think that thinking requires a brain. Indeed, thoughts can now be identified on scanning equipment. When a particular pattern appears a person can be told what it is that they are thinking at that very moment; how strange it is that when the brain is dissected all that is observed is grey stuff – the stuff that was previously identified as containing thoughts. One has to seriously reflect on the possible implications of this discovery.

This discovery has only been made because human beings have awareness and communication skills. When the human that is being scanned asserts: "I am now thinking about playing tennis", he is demonstrating both awareness of having a thought and the ability to communicate this aware-ness. If either of these capabilities were absent the discovery would have been impossible. It is the awareness and the consequent verbal report which enable the person doing the scanning to correlate the particular pattern of the grey stuff with the particular thought.

It is surely the case that there are non-human animals which have both communication skills and awareness. Would the scanning equipment be able to isolate particular thoughts in these non-human animals? It would be able to detect patterns in grey stuff – but is this pattern a thought? Knowing that it is a thought would either require either the human scanner to learn the communication framework of the non-human animal, or the non-human animal to learn the communication framework of the human scanner. Without this communication there would be an unbridgeable divide – the scanner looking at various patterns of grey stuff, and the non-human animal either having various thoughts, or having no thoughts.

Which is it? The most sensible answer seems to be that the non-human animal is having thoughts, especially when the patterns of grey stuff resemble those in the human brain in some way. Another question worth asking is: Would non-human animals be able to isolate each other's thoughts if they had the scanning equipment? Working out how to operate the equipment could be an issue, but if the design is simple there is no reason to believe that the 'scanner' through a process of association between verbal reports from the 'scanned' and observations of the 'grey-stuff patterns' couldn't make the connection. It would be a fortuitous discovery though.

It should be obvious that the identification of 'patterns of stuff' with 'thoughts' requires both awareness of the thoughts and communication skills. The 'scanner' also requires the ability to reason. Given these restrictions it is obviously exceptionally difficult to show the existence of thought in the non-human world. We come back to the question: What is a thought? It appears that a thought is a 'pattern of stuff' which is observable through scanning equipment, but which is only initially known to be a particular thought through the direct awareness of the thought.

The whole universe can be viewed as simply 'patterns of stuff'. So, one might justifiably ask: Is the whole universe having thoughts? The immediate problem with answering this question is that the universe can be divided up arbitrarily into a near-infinite number of 'patterns'. Surely, all of these patterns aren't thoughts! Of course, the brain itself could be divided up into a near infinite array of arbitrary patterns. So, the serious question is whether there are non-arbitrary 'patterns of stuff' in the universe that are 'thoughts'? Of course, we have already established that there are – in human brains. It is surely the case that there are also such non-arbitrary patterns in non-human animal brains.

Are there any other non-arbitrary patterns which could possibly be thoughts? Physical and chemical interactions are obvious candidates. When physical interactions and chemical interactions occur these are non-arbitrary patterns which could repeatedly instantiate the same thought. We are not talking about complex thoughts such as: "I wonder where my keys are – the car, the table, stolen, the pub I went to last night – oh, they are in my pocket". We are also not talking about the ability to have awareness of the thought or to communicate the thought. We are simply talking about a thought such as: "move", which is had by a hydrogen atom as it senses an oxygen atom it can interact with. Of course, the word 'move' is a human arrangement of letters, the actual thought would not be framed in language – it would be a pure impulse in response to surrounding stimuli. The external signs of the impulse would be a repeated 'pattern' observable by third parties with the appropriate equipment.

This may seem a bit extravagant. But it is surely the case that humans too have a plethora of unconscious thought impulses in response to surrounding stimuli which are simple and not framed in language. A human can think and act without language. In some instances it is only when a human is asked why they carried out a particular action that they confabulate a story about their 'thoughts' that is framed in language.

Is thought related to freedom? It surely is. It is possible that it is because humans are aware of thought that they believe themselves to have freedom. It follows from this that if humans were unaware of thought that they would not have the concept 'freedom'. They would just obliviously think and act. Their existence would be very similar to the thoughts and actions of atoms – if such thoughts exist. The only difference in humans would be the complexity of the 'patterns' and the concordant complexity of the 'thoughts'. If freedom is a delusion it is a delusion which requires a high level of 'pattern' complexity. Of course, freedom might well not be a delusion, and the majority of the universe might have freedom without having the concept of freedom.

Finally, let us reflect on a possible link between thought and the vibration patterns of 'chiming' and 'grating' that were explored in *Reflection Two*. We have seen that a thought is a particular pattern of stuff; when a new thought occurs there is a movement from one pattern of stuff to a new pattern of stuff. All movements of stuff lead to the emanation of particular vibrations of air molecules into the surroundings. Therefore, we would expect thoughts to generate 'chiming' and 'grating' effects. It is therefore encouraging that there is plenty of experimental evidence that when people are instructed to direct their thoughts and their concentration on the back of the head of another person that that person often senses the thoughts that are directed towards them.

This phenomenon is called 'the sense of being stared at' and experiments entail 'looking trials'.

Rupert Sheldrake claims that: "The scores in looking trials were positive and staggeringly significant statistically, while they were at chance levels in the non-looking trials...Dozens of independent investigators all over the world have obtained very similar patterns of results."[11] This evidence has typically been interpreted as showing that 'rays' emanate out from the eyes of one person to the back of the head of the other person. For example, Sheldrake claims that: "vision involves a two-way process: an inward movement of light and an outward projection of images"[12]. From the perspective outlined here it is directed thought and not 'eye rays' that is the cause of the documented effects.

---

[11] Sheldrake, Rupert, *The Sense of Being Stared At*, Arrow Books, London, 2003, p. 171.

[12] Sheldrake, Rupert, *The Sense of Being Stared At*, Arrow Books, London, 2003, p. 121.

Reflection 6

The Location of Sensations

Let us reflect on the location of a sensation. A location is a particular isolatable area of space-time. A sensation is a raw feel. For the sake of simplicity let us focus solely on one particular example. When my finger touches the red-hot pan that is in the oven I become aware of a sensation that I find to be not very pleasant. In order to try and cause this unpleasant sensation to cease as soon as possible I immediately submerge my finger into a bowl of ice-cold water. In doing this I become aware of another sensation that I also find to be not very pleasant. These sensations are 'raw feels'. Do these sensations have a location? If so, where is it? Is it even coherent to argue that they have no location?

Is it not obviously true that if something exists it has a location, and if something doesn't exist that it doesn't have a location? Why would anyone seek to deny such a trivial truism? Perhaps they are confused by the phrase 'has a location'. One might believe that a 'tree' has a location but that my thought: "there is a tree", has no location. The reason for believing this presumably being the belief that the thought cannot be identified and delineated with absolute precision – the thought originates in my head but it is an output of certain functional interactions. Therefore, one could argue that the interactions are located but that the thought is not; one can point at a location on a brain-scan but in doing so one is not pointing at the location of a thought. But, surely it is precisely thought which one is observing when one looks at a brain-scan whilst someone is thinking. More than this, one is observing the location of thought. Isolating the exact isolatable area of space-time which is the thought is not as easy as isolating a 'tree' – but it is possible in principle. Clearly, a thought which has never existed will not have a location.

What other factors could lead someone to believe that something exists but that it has no location? One possibility seems to be some kind of sceptical epistemological position which asserts that it is brains which create space-time, and the under-lying reality is non-spatial and non-temporal. Brains are amazing, but they are surely incapable of producing the spatial out of the non-spatial, and the temporal out of the non-temporal! Let us stay within the realms of plausibility and accept that if something exists it exists somewhere, and if something doesn't exist it doesn't exist anywhere.

Let us not be distracted from our objective by views such as the following: "When I observe a person groaning and writhing about on the floor in a pool of blood he is in pain. The person as a whole is in pain but the sensations he is feeling do not have a location." Here there are two disparate things going on – the ascription of 'pain' and the location of unpleasant sensations. Of course, in normal circumstances if we see such a person we will assume that they are in 'pain' – in other words, we will assume that they are aware of unpleasant sensations. Furthermore, we will assume that these sensations are located somewhere within the confines of their body. Our ascription of the label 'in pain' will obviously be incorrect if the person is acting, or if they have a rare medical condition which causes them to not experience unpleasant sensations. Our concern here is with first-person awareness of particular sensations. These sensations exist and as an existent they have a location.

So, the sensations that we are concerned with here – those relating to my finger: Where are they located? There are only three remotely plausible views. Firstly, they are located in my finger. Secondly, they are located in my brain. Thirdly, they are partially located in my finger and partially located in my brain, with the possibility that they are partially located elsewhere in my body too.

So, my finger touches the red-hot pan that is in the oven and I simultaneously become aware of a sensation that I find to be not very pleasant. The sensation certainly appears to me to be located in my finger – this is the reason I try and cause this unpleasant sensation to cease as soon as possible by immediately submerging my finger into a bowl of ice-cold water. It is the finger that came into contact with the red-hot pan so there are very good reasons for believing that this appearance is correct – that the sensation is located in the finger itself. In this view the brain simply acts as a 'register' which records the information that a sensation is located in the finger. So, when the sensation arises in my finger my brain registers the information: "there is an unpleasant sensation in my finger" – and this information will show up on a brain-scan. It seems so obvious that the sensation is located in my finger that one might be excused for wondering why the issue even needs discussing.

The reason is that many contemporary philosophers seek to argue that the body is an insensitive machine, and that all sensations must therefore be located in the brain. This is our second view. These philosophers come up with arguments to try and convince people that the finger is only the location of tissue damage and that the sensation is projected there by the brain through a process of association. So, when I see my finger touch the red hot pan, a sensation is located in my brain, and I link the two events together and fallaciously assume that the sensation is in the finger. David Armstrong claims that: "to say the sensation of heat is in the hand is only to say that we believe, or are inclined to believe, that the bodily cause of the sensation is in the hand...something necessarily distinct from the sensation, its putative cause, is in the hand".[13]

What has led philosophers to see the body as an insensitive machine? These philosophers have surely

---

[13] Armstrong, David, "Vesey on Sensations of Heat", *Australasian Journal of Philosophy* (1963), 41, p 361.

been indoctrinated into a 'world view' in which this assumption is made. This 'world view' can be characterised as 'braincentricism' – the view that sensations, awareness, thought, memory, and intelligence all require a brain for their existence; whilst all of the engulfing surroundings of brains – the 'non-brain' – have radically different qualities – they are just 'matter'. Those who are encapsulated within this 'world view' cannot comprehend how a sensation could exist unless it is located in a brain. This forces them to deny the obvious and come up with an account as to why the sensation that appears to be in the finger could possibly be in the brain.

Our third view is that the sensations we are concerned with here are partially located in my finger, partially located in my brain, and possibly located elsewhere in the body too. This possibility seems to be far more plausible than the last as it accepts that the sensation is partially located where it appears to be – where the finger touches the red-hot pan – and it doesn't assert that the body is an insensitive machine, which it is surely not. In our example the location of the sensation would stretch from the point in the finger which contacted the red-hot pan, though the hand, up the arm, through the neck and into the brain. There would effectively be a sensation 'stretched out' from the point of contact in the finger to the 'registration' area in the brain.

Let us accept that either the first view or the third view are correct, and let us see the second view as being the product of a soon to be outdated 'world view'. Sensations are located in body parts themselves. We saw in *Reflection One* that there are good reasons for believing that there is no real distinction between 'body' and 'world'; the fundamental distinction in reality being between 'awareness' and the 'body-world'. So, if sensations are located in the 'body' this also implies that they are located in the 'world'. Indeed, this is simply a repetition of the conclusion we reached in *Reflection One*. There we concluded that raw feels (qualia) most likely exist throughout the 'undifferentiated' and precede 'awareness'. Whilst here we now conclude that raw feels (sensations) are located throughout the 'body-world'. The 'undifferentiated' and the 'body-world' are one. 'Raw feels', 'qualia' and 'sensations' are also one. Furthermore, returning to *Reflection Two*, we can also conclude that 'raw feels', 'qualia', 'sensations', and 'chiming' / 'grating' are one.

Reflection 7

Character and Personality

The words 'character' and 'personality' have been created by humans to refer to an attribute of humans.[14] Whilst the words are two, the attribute is one. What exactly is this attribute? Does the attribute exist in a human before they are born? Do 'non-human animals' have this attribute? Does all of the undifferentiated have this attribute?

It is surely the case that if only one 'animal' – a sole human – had ever come into existence they wouldn't have considered themselves as having character. It is the observation of other humans and the fact that in seemingly identical situations different humans act very differently that leads to the concept of 'character'. When a twenty pound note is placed on the floor of a library one human is observed putting it in their pocket, leaving the

---

[14] Of course, the word 'humans' refers to a vaguely similar set of 'patterns of movements' within the undifferentiated.

library and buying a bottle of whisky. Another human is observed handing the note to the librarian. The inference is drawn that the disparity in these actions occurs because the two humans have different characters.

One initial problem with this inference is that there is, in reality, no such thing as two identical situations. The supposed identity is a mere 'seeming'. A complete analysis of a particular situation would require a microscopic analysis of all of the engulfing surroundings of the humans at the moment of action. Let us define character as 'the particular way an entity responds in a particular situation'. Even if we postulate the possibility of two identical characters existing, then they will still never encounter identical situations. This means that differences in character cannot be used to account for differences in action in seemingly identical situations. The explanation of difference in action could be difference in actual situation.

Of course, the situation is much more intricate than this. When we expand our focus from a particular situation to sequences of situations, we find that the actions of a human in a particular situation are determined not just by a microscopic analysis of these engulfing surroundings, but also by every single set of engulfing surroundings that they have ever encountered in their life. Sets of engulfing surroundings both forge future actions and determine present actions. Given that every set of engulfing surroundings is unique, and that every set plays a role in forging character, it follows that the existence of two identical characters is impossible.

Let us return to the library scenario. We are correct to assert that the two humans have different characters. However, their difference in action cannot be used as evidence for this. We can hypothesize that the two humans have identical characters and had encountered identical sets of engulfing surroundings their entire lives up to the point where they entered the library, and therefore had acted identically in all of these surroundings. Nevertheless, a single change in the engulfing surroundings that exist in the library – the first such difference they had ever encountered – could explain their difference in action. From this moment on the two humans will have different characters.

This hypothetical situation, in which identical characters are postulated, is a useful tool. However, the question remains as to whether the attribute of 'character' exists in a human before they are born. Is character partially inherited or purely acquired from engulfing surroundings? Or does this question itself assume a false dichotomy?

There is clearly no such thing as an environment-independent character – the notion is utterly vacuous. The life of a particular organism needs to be viewed as a long sequence of individual sets of movements in response to particular environments. A particular organism will inherit from its parent/s the disposition to act in a certain way if it encounters certain environments. Offspring generally encounter surrounding environments which are very similar to those that their parent/s encountered and so exhibit similar characters – that is to say, they exhibit similar movements in response to these environments – to their parents. So, when living organisms reproduce, their offspring need to be envisioned as repetitions of slightly different sets of movements in response to very similar engulfing surroundings.

The lack of environment-independent 'character' means that the distinction often made between 'nurture' and 'nature' is a false dichotomy. There is no such thing as 'nurture' that is independent of 'nature'. All that is acquired by offspring is a set of dispositions to movement in particular environments (this includes 'thought' which is the result of particular movements in the brain in response to particular environments). These dispositions only become translated into character if the particular environments are encountered. Character doesn't exist prior to the encountering of these surroundings. All differences in surroundings will lead to differences in character. It is only because offspring encounter similar engulfing surroundings to their parent/s that they often demonstrate similar 'characters' to their parents.

I have argued that is the observation of other humans and the way that they act (make different movements) in response to seemingly similar sets of surroundings that leads to the concept of 'character'. Character is simply 'the particular way an entity responds in a particular situation'. It is because one cannot observe the intricate movements going on inside the brains of humans that their movements are usually unpredictable to us. When we spend a lot of time with a particular human we get to know how they respond to particular sets of similar surroundings. That is to say, we get to know which movements in their brain and body are likely to occur in response to a particular environment. No two sets of engulfing surroundings are identical so however well we know a human we will sometimes be surprised by their movements.

The unobservable nature of movements within brains combined with the immense number of interactions that occur in brains can give the impression that humans are a unique part of reality – a part that is unpredictable due to the presence of 'character' and 'freedom'. What a false impression this is. Character is simply 'the particular way an entity responds in a particular situation'. So, all parts of the undifferentiated have character. The universe is simply a mass of stuff which responds to itself in a particular way given the particular situation that exists. There is no distinction between the metabolising undifferentiated and the non-metabolising undifferentiated in terms of 'character'. In other words, it is not the case that only life-forms have 'character'. After all, the separation of the metabolising undifferentiated from the undifferentiated as a whole requires a perceiver. The undifferentiated is a complex web of movements and every movement is a demonstration of 'character'.

The reason why many might think that 'character' is a unique attribute of humans, or humans and a few other 'species', is simply that human movements appear to be unpredictable whilst movements of things such as the 'planets' in the sky above appear to be predictable. However, in the undifferentiated everything has 'character'.

Reflection 8

The Evolution of Humans from their Surroundings

These are a series of reflections on humans and their engulfing surroundings. One of the central issues is clearly the issue of the evolution of humans from these surroundings. It is only in the past hundred and fifty years that it has started to be increasingly recognized that humans have evolved from their surroundings. Some humans have experienced a radical change in their 'world view' as they have fully comprehended this fact; others are indoctrinated into the fact but rarely ponder its significance in any depth. Increasing realization of the implications of this fact will shape the path of human 'world views' far into the future.

When we look at the evolution of humans from the metabolising undifferentiated it was Charles Darwin who established beyond any reasonable doubt that this occurs. He demonstrated that species are not fixed but arise out of and develop into other species. In other words, all of the metabolising undifferentiated has a common ancestor. In the distant past all that existed was the 'non-metabolising undifferentiated' – the movements in the undifferentiated didn't include metabolising movements. Then the first 'metabolising movements' originated within the undifferentiated – these are the first 'life-forms' which gave rise to the plethora of metabolising movements that have existed since through common descent. This theory of evolution by common descent is now generally accepted as a brute fact in most 'world views'.

In more recent times the focus has shifted to the totality of the surroundings engulfing humans – the 'undifferentiated'. There is evidence for the view that all of these engulfing surroundings – and obviously humans themselves – originated in a Big Bang. Here we are not talking about the evolution of humans from other life-forms; we are talking about the evolution of humans from 'non-life' – evolution of humans from the 'non-metabolising undifferentiated'.

If one fully comprehends the process of evolution from Big Bang to human then there is plenty to reflect about. Which attributes of humans are also attributes of all of the surroundings engulfing humans? Which attributes of humans are also attributes of all of the 'metabolising undifferentiated? The vast majority of 'world views' envision humans as having many attributes which are uniquely human – attributes which are not shared by the engulfing surroundings. A few 'world views' grant some of these attributes to 'human-like' non-human animals. It has been one of the objectives of the reflections presented here to seriously consider the likelihood that many of the attributes typically considered to be uniquely human are actually pervasive in the surroundings engulfing humans.

Let us accept that all life-forms have a common ancestor, the evidence is overwhelming. But let us also accept that we are ignorant of the mechanisms and forces underlying the movements in both the 'non-metabolising undifferentiated' and the metabolising undifferentiated' which first gave rise to life, and then caused one species to develop into another. The evidence for the fact of evolution is not evidence for the mechanism underlying evolution.

If the attributes of thought, character, memory, experience, qualia, and the capacity to be 'chimed' and 'grated' exist throughout the undifferentiated, then it surely these factors that are the dominant force underlying the movements within the undifferentiated which we call 'evolution'.

Reflection 9

The Place of Humans in the Evolution of their Surroundings

Humans have evolved from their surroundings. Humans are particular sets of movements within the 'metabolising undifferentiated'. The 'metabolising undifferentiated' can also be referred to by the phrase 'life as a whole'. 'Life as a whole' is therefore a term which refers to the movements within the undifferentiated which are metabolising movements. The undifferentiated has always contained a vast array of movements but it took a long time to evolve 'metabolising movements'; that is to say, it took a long time to evolve the movements that humans segregate and call 'life'. The question before us here is the following: Does the particular set of movements that is 'human movements' have a special place in the evolution of the undifferentiated?

One possibility is that the undifferentiated interacts with itself in such a way as to give rise to a sequence of transitions in 'movements' which inevitably lead to humans. Initially there were only non-metabolising movements. Interactions between non-metabolising movements gave rise to the simple metabolising movements which we call 'plants'. These movements then gave rise to the more pronounced metabolising movements which we call 'animals'. Finally, the metabolising movements of non-human animals gave rise to the unique metabolising movements which we call 'human'.

The other possibility is that the undifferentiated interacts with itself in a less directed manner. In this scenario the emergence of metabolising movements was fortuitous, and the evolution of humans is immensely fortuitous. The transitions within the 'metabolising undifferentiated' are here envisioned as being determined purely by which particular sets of movements adapt best to the environment and have the most offspring. If one accepts this natural selection scenario in its typical formulation then there is no reason to believe that humans have a special place in the evolution of the undifferentiated.

We have seen that there is overwhelming evidence that humans have evolved from their surroundings, but negligible evidence concerning the mechanism underlying evolution. This means that coherent arguments can be made for both of the above possibilities. The possibility that the undifferentiated interacts with itself in such a way as to inevitably lead to the metabolising movements we call 'human' is not a contemporarily fashionable view. To many it seems to be both a religious view and to be contradicted by scientific evidence. Of course, they are wrong on both counts. There is nothing 'religious' or 'unscientific' about the assertion that the undifferentiated interacts with itself through a mechanism which leads to various transitions between 'movement types' that inevitably leads to the 'metabolising movements' of the type we call 'human'.

Let us explore this contemporarily unfashionable view. It is an unfashionable view because many now see humans as fundamentally 'just another animal'. This view is opposed to the older religious views which see humans as 'special' – as having dominion over other animals. Surely people say, if humans are at their very core 'just another animal' then how can he justifiably have dominion over non-human animals? How can humans be 'special'? This opposition which has been created is surely a false one. Humans can be fundamentally 'just another animal', but also be 'special' and have dominion over the non-human. In other words, the metabolising movements of humans can be both the movements of an animal and also a very special type of movement – a movement possessed by no other animal, and a movement possessed by no other part of the undifferentiated.

Let us explore why this is so. Let us explore why the surroundings engulfing humans could have interacted with themselves in a particular way in order to give rise to humans. Our first area of interest has to be the origin of metabolising movements – the origin of life. Let us make the widespread assumption that in the past there was a time when the only movements in the undifferentiated were non-metabolising movements. Then at a particular moment the first metabolising movement originated in the undifferentiated. The question before us is: Was this origination a fluke? Or, contrarily: Is the undifferentiated seeking to bring forth metabolising movements whenever and wherever it possibly can? Metabolising movements exist on the Earth because the conditions were favourable for their origination and propagation.

The conditions on our neighbouring planets are less favourable. Let us accept the most convincing explanation for this – wherever conditions allow the undifferentiated brings forth metabolising movements.

What happens when metabolising movements arise? Our only knowledge of what happens comes from the history of the Earth. Initially the movements are very limited in their scope and only exist in what we call 'bacteria'. In time the bacteria interacted both with themselves and with the non-metabolising undifferentiated in order to give rise to more complex movements such as those we call 'eukaryotic cells' and 'algae'. The question which needs to be asked is why did this occur? Is it the case that just as the undifferentiated seeks to bring forth metabolising movements, so simple metabolising movements seek to bring forth more diverse and complex metabolising movements? Why would this be the case? Clearly a greater array of movement patterns brings with it an increased likelihood that some of these patterns will survive if the surroundings which engulf the metabolising undifferentiated markedly change.

In other words, once the undifferentiated successfully brings forth metabolising movements these movements diversify and complexify in an attempt to maintain themselves. If they don't maintain themselves then the undifferentiated has only had a transitory success in its attempt to bring forth metabolising movements. Every life-form that has ever existed is a unique pattern of metabolising movements, which through its uniqueness aids the chances of survival of 'life as a whole'.

Looking at the fossil record we can see clear evidence that the complexity of 'metabolising movement patterns' has increased in stages. Simple 'bacteria' combined to form the 'eukaryotic cell', which in turn combined to form 'plants'. 'Plants' while themselves bringing forth an increase in 'metabolising movement patterns' also enabled the bringing forth of a vast array of much more intricate patterns of movements – those of 'animals'. Consider the pattern of metabolising movements that we call a 'cheetah'. As the 'cheetah' runs at full speed across the surface of the Earth there exists a highly complex set of metabolising movements in this area of space-time. Every cell in this area of space-time is metabolising as it glides across the surface of the Earth. There exists a plethora of intricate metabolising movements in what we call the 'brain' of the 'cheetah' as it perceives the metabolising movements which are its prey. Every area of what we call the 'organs' or 'body parts' of the 'cheetah' are unique sets of metabolising movements.

A 'cheetah' is clearly a much more complex 'metabolising movement pattern' than an 'oak tree'. 'Plants' have brought forth 'cheetahs'; metabolising movements have complexified. Fair enough one might say, but why are 'humans' special? Surely the metabolising movement pattern of 'human' is very similar to that of a 'cheetah' – not of a difference in kind. But of course the pattern of 'human' is special. Whilst 'plants' are rooted to the surface of the Earth, the patterns of 'non-human animals' can be found moving around on the surface of the Earth and moving around in the atmosphere of the Earth. In contrast, the patterns of humans extend beyond the boundaries of the planetary atmosphere. This is why the metabolising movement pattern of humans is very special.

Let us recap. It has been argued that the undifferentiated seeks to bring forth metabolising patterns wherever conditions allow. Once they arise metabolising patterns seek to survive through complexifying. The metabolising pattern of that part of the undifferentiated we call 'humans' is the objective of this process as this pattern extends outside the planetary atmosphere and thereby enables the metabolising movements to survive when their originating planet becomes inhospitable for metabolising movements. The undifferentiated seeks to bring forth metabolising movements and then to sustain the existence of these movements.

In other words, there is an inherent drive within the undifferentiated to give rise to the metabolising movements we call 'life' and then for these movements to complexify and ripple out through their engulfing surroundings as much as possible. In this process of evolution the metabolising movement of 'humans' is a key movement as it is the movement, aided by technology, in which 'life' ripples out from its host planet to more distant surroundings.

Reflection 10

Technology and the Environmental Crisis

Let us reflect on technology and the environmental crisis. Technology is part of the non-metabolising undifferentiated; it is part of the non-metabolising undifferentiated which is brought forth on Earth by 'humans'. The pervasiveness and advanced nature of technology since the industrial revolution has had a number of effects. These include a range of modifications to the planetary environment that many claim are initiating a human-induced 'environmental crisis' – these are chiefly *climate change* which arises from extensive fossil fuel use and deforestation; and, an *increasing loss of biodiversity* arising from an over-exploitation of resources and habitat modification.

There are still a minority of humans who deny that the human species has significantly altered the planetary environmental conditions. This view seems to be obviously wrong – there is adequate scientific knowledge of how the atmosphere and carbon dioxide sinks work to know for certain that humanity has significantly changed the environment. In fact, it is not even a question of science. It is simply a brute fact that every living thing modifies its environment in virtue of being a pattern of metabolising movements. And it also straightforwardly follows that humanity has *increasingly* modified the planetary environment throughout recent history because of two incontrovertible factors – the human population explosion, and the increasing use of technology.

Having said this, let us consider how technology and the 'environmental crisis' relate to the claim that the 'metabolising movement pattern' that is 'the human species' is the objective of 'life as a whole'. When the undifferentiated gives rise to the 'metabolising undifferentiated' the act of metabolism itself can be thought of as 'tool use'. When metabolism originated the metabolising undifferentiated used the non-metabolising undifferentiated to maintain itself; it used it as a 'tool'. As pattern complexity increased metabolising entities utilised both the non-metabolising undifferentiated and other parts of the metabolising undifferentiated to maintain themselves. As pattern complexity increased further metabolising entities purposefully moulded the non-metabolising undifferentiated into 'external tools' which could be repeatedly used. The final stage of pattern complexity is 'the human species' which moulds the non-metabolising undifferentiated into complex technology. It is the very bringing forth of this technology that makes the metabolising pattern of the human species so special – it is technology that enables the metabolising pattern of the human species to extend outside the planetary atmosphere.

So, technological progress can be viewed as a crucial part of the strivings of 'life as a whole' as it seeks to maintain itself in existence. How is the 'environmental crisis' of modernity to be viewed from this perspective? From this perspective the changes that the human species have made to the environment are neither good nor bad; they simply reflect the nature of the metabolising undifferentiated, and its strivings to survive.

This might strike one as slightly odd as it is generally held that the human species is the *cause* of a global environmental crisis that will lead to a mass extinction of species, including in all likelihood the human species itself. Scientists tell us that when the environment is disrupted too much several 'tipping points' will be passed and planetary climatic conditions will jump to a new more stable set – a set that is not conducive for the continued existence of the human species and many others.

However, from the wider perspective of viewing technological progress from the viewpoint of 'life as a whole', it can be seen that these scientists miss the bigger picture. From this perspective it can be seen that the human species is not the initiator of harm to the rest of life, it is the metabolising movement pattern that is the saviour of life.

In the bigger scheme of things the environmental changes predicted to occur in the 'environmental crisis' of modernity are trivial. In the bigger picture the homeostatic regulatory capacity of the biosphere is already under serious strain. This has nothing to do with humans but simply follows from planetary astrobiology.

Planets are born, some go though phases where they can support life, and at least one (the Earth) has gone through a stage where life evolves to a stage where it regulates the environmental conditions of the planet in order to maintain itself. Then, inevitably, the conditions for survival become less favourable as the output of the sun continuously increases and the homeostatic regulatory capacity therefore weakens. At this stage a technological 'species' is required to manage the planetary environment and to bring forth metabolising movement patterns which, via the non-metabolising movements we call 'technology', enable life to leave the planet. If this does not occur then first complex metabolising movements go out of existence as the planetary homeostatic regulatory capacity weakens, and then all 'life' becomes extinguished from the planet as the ever-increasing output of the sun becomes too much for even simple metabolising movements to survive.

This is the bigger picture. The environmental changes which are referred to as the 'environmental crisis' are the initial stage of the technological control of planetary conditions. The part of the undifferentiated that is 'life as a whole' is moulding the undifferentiated into complex movements (technology) via the metabolising movements we call 'humans' in order to regulate planetary conditions and thereby ensure its survival.

Reflection 11

Science versus Faith

There is a place for both science and faith. Maintaining faith in something that is flatly contradicted by science is inappropriate. However, asserting that science has all the answers and that one shouldn't have faith in things which have not been established by science is clearly even more inappropriate. In fact, given that the scientific endeavour originated such a short time ago it wouldn't just be inappropriate – it would be utterly ridiculous.

Let us return to the case of evolution. Many people maintain a 'world view' which flatly contradicts the fact of evolution and the geological evidence of the age of the Earth. In this instance their faith seems to be misplaced. However, those people who champion evolution overstep the mark by believing that science has established things which it hasn't established. Let us accept that evolution is a fact – all of the life-forms that exist today originated from a common ancestor. There is a mass of evidence that this is so. Let us not accept that an adequate scientific account has been given for the mechanism underlying this fact. There is negligible evidence that natural selection gives rise to speciation. The champions of evolution usually confuse the two. They mistake the evidence of the fact of evolution for evidence of natural selection. It is clearly possible that there is some 'intelligence' or 'guiding force' in the universe which underpins the evolutionary process. The evidence for the fact of evolution is not evidence against this position. Even if there were convincing evidence that natural selection plays some kind of role in speciation that would not be evidence against this position. Having faith in such a force is entirely appropriate.

Let us look at the case of prayer. This is a good example of the appropriate boundaries between science and faith. There is a widespread belief in the effectiveness of prayer. If a loved one is taken ill with a potentially life-threatening condition it is normal for people to pray for them. Those who are wholly 'scientific' ridicule such activities. When a prominent advocate of science and natural selection was unfortunately taken seriously ill his friends prayed for him. On recovering rather than thanking them he remarked: "Did you also sacrifice a goat?"

A wise person will clearly see that science is in its infancy and provides no reason whatsoever to believe that prayer for loved ones is ineffective. A plausible mechanism for the transmission and effectiveness of prayers exists. The 'vibration frequencies' generated by the act of prayer could be 'chiming' frequencies that resonate with their surroundings. Given quantum entanglement it would be expected that these 'chiming' frequencies are preferentially transmitted to those surroundings which the person who is praying is most deeply embedded with. These surroundings will include loved ones. So, if lots of people start praying for a loved one they could become 'chimed' rather than 'grated', and this could aid their recovery.

So, it is entirely appropriate to have faith in the effectiveness of prayer, and a good thing to have lots of caring friends. Whether the proposed mechanism operates exactly as specified is not important. What is important is that such a mechanism is possible and people shouldn't seek to deny this in the name of science. When science oversteps its domain it is unhelpful – it causes an unnecessary clash with faith, which can cause those with faith to doubt firmly established science.

If I become seriously ill I hope people pray for me.

Reflecting on the Reflections

A 'World View' for the Future?

We have reflected on many issues and can simply conclude that the phenomena of character, thought, raw feels of 'chiming' and 'grating', and memory, could exist in all of the surroundings which engulf humans.

These surroundings, and humans themselves, are the 'undifferentiated'; distinct objects do not exist unless they are directly perceived as such. All that exists is undifferentiated stuff and differentiable but unobservable awareness. The undifferentiated stuff itself is a vast intertwined web of diverse 'movement patterns' in which raw feels and experiences intermingle throughout. When 'awareness' (a 'point of access') emerges it becomes aware of some of these raw feels through events such as 'grating' and 'chiming', and the event of the finger touching the red-hot pan. It also becomes aware of non-qualia experiences such as 'observing a tree'.

Most 'points of access' to the undifferentiated are 'clouded' but they are sometimes 'unclouded'. This means that an 'awareness' can, in principle, become aware of the sensations, memories, and thoughts, that originate in any part of the undifferentiated. Of course, the majority of movement patterns we call 'human' would have difficulty accepting that some of the sensations, memories, and thoughts that are in their awareness originated and exist outside their 'bodies'. We have seen that it is easier for 'unclouded' 'points of access' such as infants and the 'medium', and becomes starkly obvious in the case of organ transplantation.

We have concluded that humans evolved from the undifferentiated and have a very special role within the undifferentiated. If memory, raw feels of 'chiming' and 'grating', character, and thought, exist throughout the undifferentiated, then they would surely be the prime factors shaping the entire evolutionary process from Big Bang to 'human'.

Having said all this let us return to, and reflect on, our opening quotes:

Nothing ever is, everything is becoming.

Knowing ignorance is strength. Ignoring knowledge is sickness.

'World views' evolve, they are a part of everything, and everything is in a state of becoming. 'World views' evolve as knowledge increases. There will always be humans who ignore knowledge because it clashes with their existing 'world view'. Here we have explored new avenues of knowledge, and new perspectives on that knowledge, which may shape the dominant 'world views' of the future.

However, realisation that everything is in a state of becoming means that we need to also acknowledge our ignorance, and accept that even future 'world views' will be superseded. This is the inevitability of eternal becoming.